SENT BY THE LORD
Songs of the World Church
VOLUME 2

edited & arranged by John L. Bell

WILD GOOSE PUBLICATIONS
Iona Community
GLASGOW

First published 1991

To
Pablo Sosa
and
Musica Para Todos

Design:
Graham Maule.

Cover photograph:
Dougie Small.

The Wild Goose is a Celtic symbol of the Holy Spirit.
It is the trademark of Wild Goose Publications.

© Copyright 1991 Iona Community/Wild Goose Publications
ISBN 0 947988 44 0

Wild Goose Publications
The Publishing Division of the Iona Community
Pearce Institute, 840 Govan Road, Glasgow G51 3UU
Scotland
☎ (041) 445 − 4561

CONTENTS

- 7   INTRODUCTION
- 9   SONGS OF THE WORLD CHURCH
- 75   ACKNOWLEDGEMENTS
- 76   COPYRIGHT HOLDERS
- 79   INDEX OF FIRST LINES

THE SONGS

ARGENTINA
10   El cielo canta   (Heaven is singing for joy)

BOLIVIA
12   Sarantañani   (Let's walk together)

BRAZIL
14   Cantai ao Senhor   (O sing to the Lord)

CANADA
16   Jesous Ahatonhia   ('Twas in the moon of wintertime)

CHINA
20   Wen Ti   (May the Lord)

GERMANY
22   Gelobt sei deine Treu   (When morning meets our eyes)

GREECE
24   Kyrie eleison   (Lord, have mercy)

KOREA
26   Come now, O Prince of peace
28   Look and learn

NICARAGUA
32   Sent by the Lord am I
36   Somos pueblo que camina   (For the world and all its people)

PARAGUAY
38   Kyrie Guarany   (On the poor)

PERU
40   Gloria   (Glory to God)

PHILIPPINES
42   Let heaven your wonders proclaim
46   Loving Creator
50   Maranatha   (We believe)
52   The earth is the Lord's

PUERTO RICA
54   Alabanza   (Nourished by the rainfall)

SOUTH AFRICA
58   Alleluia
60   Bayavuya   (Your people are happy today)
62   Re ya mathematha   (We are running)
66   Senzeni na   (What have we done?)
68   Thuma mina   (Send me, Lord)

TAIWAN
70   Ch'iu Chu lienmin women   (Lord, have mercy)

ZIMBABWE
72   If you believe and I believe

COPYRIGHT

All translations of original texts and arrangements of original music are copyright the Iona Community.

While every effort has been made to identify the sources and copyright holders of materials included, the compilers would be grateful to know of information which may help to rectify details of origin etc.

Where copyright holders have been identified, the appropriate proportion of copyright fee recovered from the sale of this book will be sent to them. Where no copyright holder has been identified, the appropriate proportion of the copyright fee will be sent to the Council of Churches in the designated country.

INTRODUCTION

When we published Book One (*Many and Great*) of this series, we had no idea that the response would be so positive. Not only did people get in touch saying how much they appreciated having access to such material and how much they enjoyed using it, but we were also sent wads of manuscript and copies of hymnaries and song books from all over the world. At present we are slowly, but appreciatively, wading our way through them to glean more for future publications.

Like *Many and Great*, this is an eclectic collection. There is no specific theme. The songs range from the first Canadian Christmas carol to a recent Zimbabwean protest song.

It will be noted, however, that a good proportion of the songs come from Central and Southern America. This is quite intentional.

1992 commemorates the "discovery" of America by Christopher Columbus. For many people in Central and Southern America, this is not a time for joy, but a time for deep regret as that occasion calls to mind the succession of waves of colonial, religious and financial imperialism which has beleaguered many of the countries in the sub-continent right to the present day.

It is therefore hoped that some of the songs in *Sent by the Lord* may be used as an antidote to the triumphalism which western countries may be tempted to associate with the centenary.

But it is also hoped that these songs, as the previous ones, will find their way into the worship of churches in Britain, be that in sanctuaries or house groups. These are the songs of the people, not of the professionals, and they can help us to celebrate God's affection for the ordinary.

John L. Bell
Wild Goose Worship Group
Glasgow.
Pentecost 1991.

A companion cassette which includes all songs in this collection is available. Entitled *Sent By The Lord*, it was recorded by the Wild Goose Worship Group and may be purchased from retailers or Wild Goose Publications.

SONGS OF THE WORLD CHURCH

EL CIELO CANTA

ARGENTINA

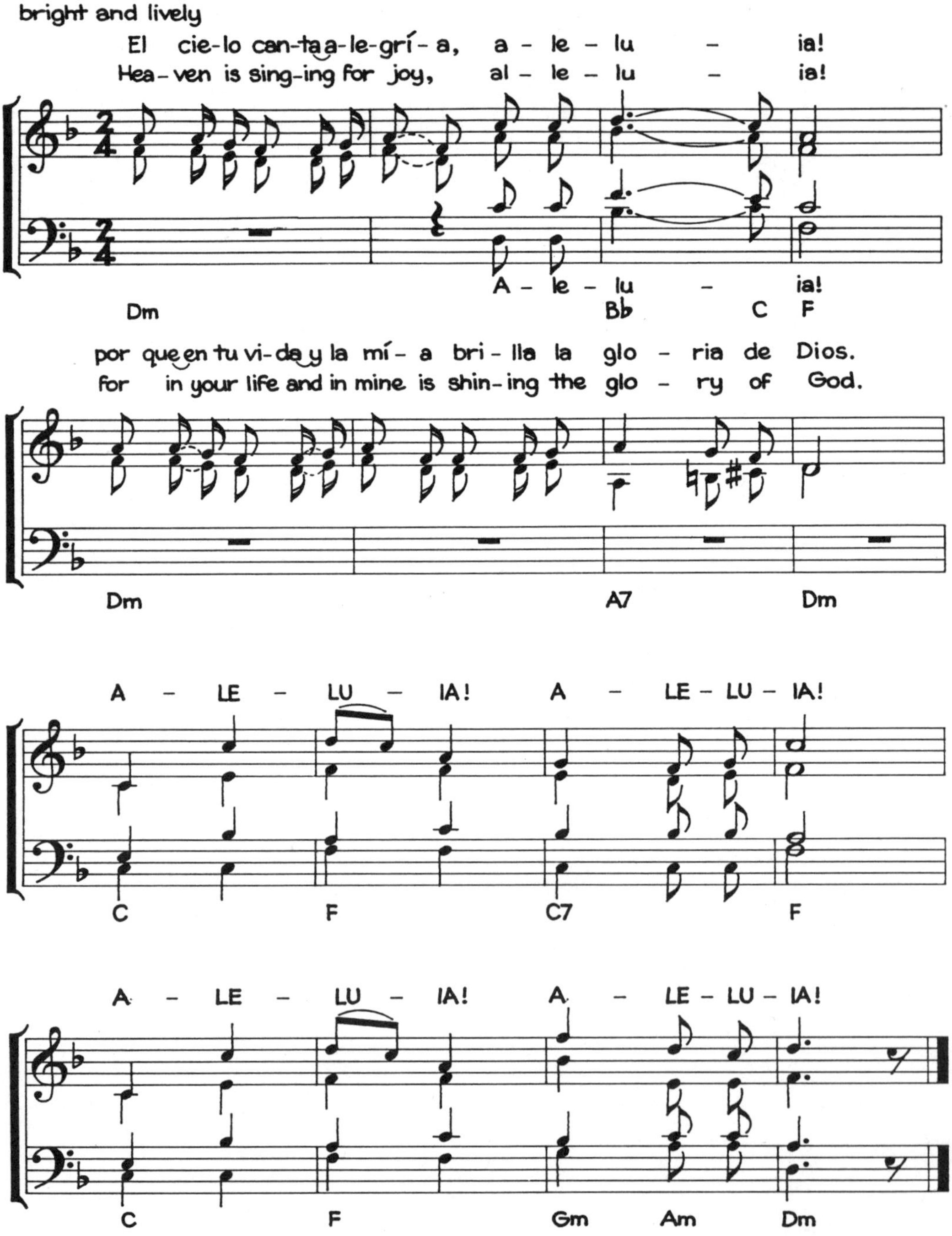
bright and lively
El cie-lo can-ta a-le-grí-a, a - le - lu - ia!
Hea-ven is sing-ing for joy, al - le - lu - ia!
A - le - lu - ia!
Dm Bb C F
por que en tu vi-da y la mí - a bri - lla la glo - ria de Dios.
for in your life and in mine is shin-ing the glo - ry of God.
Dm A7 Dm
A - LE - LU - IA! A - LE - LU - IA!
C F C7 F
A - LE - LU - IA! A - LE - LU - IA!
C F Gm Am Dm

1. *El cielo canta alegría, aleluia!*
   por que en tu vida y la mía brilla la gloria de Dios.

   ALELUIA! ALELUIA!
   ALELUIA! ALELUIA!

2. *El cielo canta alegría, aleluia!*
   porque a tu vida y la mía las une el amor de Dios.

3. *El cielo canta alegría, aleluia!*
   por que tu vida y la mía proclamarán al Señor.

1. **Heaven is singing for joy, alleluia!**
   for in your life and in mine is shining the glory of God.

2. **Heaven is singing for joy, alleluia!**
   for your life and mine unite in the love of the Lord.

3. **Heaven is singing for joy, alleluia!**
   for your life and mine will always bear witness to God.

This is a song of praise with guts. It was first heard sung simply to a guitar accompaniment and then with a piano providing bass arpeggios with a ♩ ♩ rhythm. When instruments are being used, they should, in the final bar of the words and for two after, play Dm followed on the last quaver beat by Am, ending with a triple strummed Dm in the last bar. The four part vocal arrangement is of Scottish origin.

Words : © 1991 Pablo Sosa.
Music : © 1991 Pablo Sosa;
arrangement © 1991 Iona Community.

SARANTAÑANI
BOLIVIA

positively and brightly

Ta - ta - na - ca, ma - ma - na - ca, Sa-ran - ta - ña - ni! Way - na - na - ka, ta-wa-co-na - ka, sayt'a - si - ña - ni.

Men and wo - men, let us walk and let's walk to - ge - ther. Bro - thers, sis - ters, child-ren and youth, let's all move to - ge - ther. Fine.

Chords: Dm | Gm | C7 | F | Dm/F | Gm | Dm/A | A7 | Dm

Tatanaca, mamanaca, Sarantañani!
Waynanaka, tawaconaka, sayt' asiñani.

Take Iglesia nacasaja mayaghasiñani,
Mayaqui, takeni, Sarantañani.

Men and women, let us walk
and let's walk together.
Brothers, sisters, children and youth,
Let's all move together.

Let the Church be one strong body,
walking together;
every member touched by each other,
keeping together.

The Aymara people are part of the fastest growing church in Bolivia, Southern America. They — who have their own language — took over the Methodist Church and indigenised it. This kind of crisis for the church is what must be expected if you speak about the rights of native people.

The song goes to a dance rhythm and was indeed danced at a recent meeting of the South American Council of Churches.

N.B. The English translation is more of a paraphrase to prevent what might otherwise seem like bland words — something which would be an insult to the original.

The guitar chords are not totally consonant with the harmonised arrangement.

Words :   © 1991 Zoilo Yanapa.
Music :   © 1991 Zoilo Yanapa;
arrangement © 1991 Iona Community.

CANTAI AO SENHOR
BRAZIL

Cantai ao Senhor um cantico novo,
cantai ao Senhor um cantico novo,
cantai ao Senhor um cantico novo,
cantai ao Senhor, cantai ao Senhor.

O sing to the Lord, O sing God a new song,
O sing to the Lord, O sing God a new song,
O sing to the Lord, O sing God a new song,
O sing to the Lord, O sing to the Lord.

No biographical details are available about this song or its composer. It almost certainly seems to be a Brazilian folk tune which lends itself very appropriately to the words from the Psalm, *O sing a new song to the Lord*.

Words : from Psalm 98.
Music : traditional;
© Editora Sinodal, Sao Leopoldo;
arrangement © 1991 Iona Community.

JESOUS AHATONHIA
CANADA

1. 'Twas in the moon of wintertime
   when all the birds had fled,
   that mighty Gitchi Manitou
   sent angel choirs instead;
   before their light the stars grew dim
   and wand'ring hunters heard the hymn:
   'JESUS YOUR KING IS BORN,
    JESUS IS BORN: IN EXCELSIS GLORIA!'

2. Within a lodge of broken bark
   the tender babe was found,
   a ragged rope of rabbit skin
   enwrapped his beauty 'round;
   and as the hunter braves drew nigh
   the angel song rang loud and high:
   'JESUS YOUR KING IS BORN,
    JESUS IS BORN: IN EXCELSIS GLORIA!'

3. The earliest moon of wintertime
   is not so round and fair
   as was the ring of glory on
   the helpless Infant there.
   The chiefs from far before Him knelt
   with gifts of fox and beaver pelt.
   'JESUS YOUR KING IS BORN,
    JESUS IS BORN; IN EXCELSIS GLORIA!'

4. O children of the forest free,
   O sons of Manitou,
   the Holy Child of earth and heaven
   is born today for you.
   Come kneel before the radiant Boy
   who brings you beauty, peace and joy.
   'JESUS YOUR KING IS BORN,
    JESUS IS BORN: IN EXCELSIS GLORIA!'

This is widely regarded as Canada's first Christmas carol. It was written by a Jesuit priest in the language of the Huron Indians, and uses terms familiar to the tribe to let the story of the incarnation become real in their context. The tune is from France and, when the carol is sung in the English translation, it identifies the three major cultures which have shaped contemporary Canadian life.

Words : (in Huron) Fr. Jean de Brebuf SJ, 1641;
English translation by J.E. Middleton, 1926;
© Frederick Harris Music Co. Ltd.
Music : French traditional;
arrangement © 1991 Iona Community.

WEN TI
CHINA

gracefully

May the Lord, might-y God, bless and keep you for-ev-er; grant you peace, per-fect peace, cou-rage in eve-ry en-dea-vour.

Lift up and see his face, his grace for
Lift up your eyes and see his face and his grace for

ev-er; may the Lord, might-y
ev-er; may the Lord, might-y

May the Lord, mighty God,
bless and keep you forever;
grant you peace, perfect peace,
courage in every endeavour.

Lift up your eyes and see his face,
and his grace forever;
may the Lord, mighty God,
bless and keep you forever.

This is a very beautiful song, which may be used at weddings, baptisms or on other occasions when a congregation wishes to ask for a particular blessing on individuals.

It is, of course, not essential to sing the second part for verse 2, but its inclusion helps to indicate the Far Eastern texture of the music.

Words: traditional liturgical text.
Music: of Chinese origin;
adapted by I-to Loh;
© 1983 Abingdon Press from *Hymns From The Four Winds*.

GELOBT SEI DEINE TREU
GERMANY

Gelobt sei deine Treu,
die alle Morgen neu
die alle Morgen neu.

When morning meets our eyes
and light for life supplies,
let God's eternal love be praised.

or 'Glory to God on high,'
sing angels in the sky,
'and peace on earth to those God blesses.'

The original German words come from a hymn by Joachim Klepper, a pastor in the Confessing Church and a revered hymnwriter who, with his family, was executed in Auschwitz concentration camp during World War II.

It is important not to start too low as the bottom G is as difficult for trebles as the top D is for lower voices.

The English text given is not a direct translation of the German, but offers words in a comparable sentiment. The alternative *Gloria* is particularly appropriate at Christmas time.

Words : Joachim Klepper.
Music : source unknown.

KYRIE ELEISON
GREECE

Kyrie eleison.

Lord, have mercy.

Some Orthodox music is rather difficult for western ears to assimilate, sometimes because of the elaboration of the melodic line. This is not the case with this simple *Kyrie*.

For variety, an *isom* or drone by male voices on the note D can be used to accompany trebles singing the melody. This device has the curious effect of engaging those humming the *isom* in the chant in a more fulfilling way than if all were to sing the tune.

Words :   traditional liturgical text.
Music :   *Mount Athos Melody*, traditional.

COME NOW, O PRINCE OF PEACE
KOREA

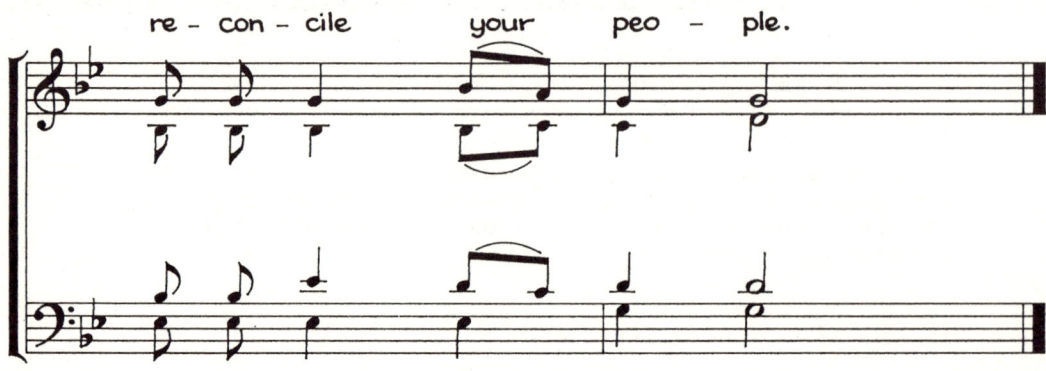

1. Come now, O Prince of peace,
   make us one body,
   come, O Lord Jesus,
   reconcile your people.

2. Come now, O God of love,
   make us one body,
   come, O Lord Jesus,
   reconcile your people.

3. Come now and set us free,
   O God, our Saviour,
   come, O Lord Jesus,
   reconcile all nations.

4. Come, Hope of unity,
   make us one body,
   come, O Lord Jesus,
   reconcile all nations.

This is a contemporary Korean song which can be sung in unison or four parts. It has a lovely simplicity and could be used to intersperse intercessions. Note the clashes in harmony towards the end and don't be afraid of them.

Words : © 1991 Geonyong Lee;
paraphrased by Marion Pope;
altered.
Music : O-so-sŏ; © 1991 Geonyong Lee.

LOOK AND LEARN
KOREA

1. Look and learn from the birds of the air,
   flying high above worry and fear;
   neither sowing nor harvesting seed,
   yet they're given whatever they need.
   If the God of earth and heaven
   cares for birds as much as this,
   won't he care much more for you,
   if you put your trust in him?

2. Look and learn from the flowers of the field,
   bringing beauty and colour to life;
   neither sewing nor tailoring cloth,
   yet they're dressed in the finest attire.
   If the God of earth and heaven
   cares for flowers as much as this,
   won't he care much more for you
   if you put your trust in him?

3. What God wants should be our will;
   where God calls should be our goal.
   When we seek the Kingdom first,
   all we've lost is ours again.
   Let's be done with anxious thoughts,
   set aside tomorrow's cares,
   live each day that God provides
   putting all our trust in him.

Q: What links Korea, Hungary and Scotland?
A: Pentatonic melody.

This is an example of the truth of the answer. Many people on hearing the melody of *Look and Learn* played on its own have been convinced that it is a Scottish or Irish fiddle tune. The reason is simply that the melody is written in the Pentatonic or five-tone scale, which is common in the music of countries which may be culturally very dissimilar.

The harmony is not Korean: the melody only was found in the source document, but the deliberate parallel harmonies in the top parts are intended to give something of an oriental feel to the music.

Words: adapted from Matthew 6 vs. 23–34.
Music: © 1991 Nah Young – Soo;
arrangement © 1991 Iona Community.

SENT BY THE LORD
NICARAGUA

Sent by the Lord am I;
my hands are ready now
to make the earth the place
in which the kingdom comes.
Sent by the Lord am I;
my hands are ready now
to make the earth the place
in which the kingdom comes.

The angels cannot change
a world of hurt and pain
into a world of love,
of justice and of peace.
The task is mine to do,
to set it really free.
Oh, help me to obey;
help me to do your will.

This Nicaraguan song was collected from the oral tradition. Its origins are unknown, but it is yet another good example of how the folk traditions in Central America are able to produce very lively tunes in minor keys. The words suggest that it could be used as a recessional after a scriptural benediction or perhaps used during Lent to convey the sense of purpose which was in Christ.

The four-part harmony is not Nicaraguan, but was made in Scotland. Experience suggests that while a guitar accompaniment or choral setting can add to the enjoyment, neither are pre-requisites.

N.B. In some versions, the tune appears without the dotted rhythm.

Words : from the oral tradition;
translation © 1991 Jorge Maldonado.
Music : Nicaraguan traditional;
arrangement © 1991 Iona Community.

1. Somos pueblo que camina
   par la senda del dolor.
   **ACUDAMOS JUBILOSOS
   A LA CENA DEL SEÑOR.**

2. Los humildes y los pobres
   invitados son de Dios.

3. Este pan que Dios nos brinda
   alimenta nuestra unión.

4. Cristo aquí se hace presente
   al reunirnos en su amor.

5. Los sedientos de justicia
   buscan su liberación.

1. For the world and all its people
   we address our prayers to God.
   **CONFIDENTLY, ALL CAN WORSHIP
   IN THE PRESENCE OF THE LORD.**

2. All the powerless, all the hungry
   are most precious to their God.

3. For the poor, God has a purpose,
   for the desperate, a word.

4. Christ is here and Christ is stronger
   than the strength of sin or sword.

5. God will fill the earth with justice
   when our will and his accord.

Only the melody and the Spanish text of this have been traceable along with the information that it was used as a processional song in the Nicaraguan Mass. The English words are not a direct translation.

In the original Spanish, the text is very much the song of an impoverished people and it would be impossible for most British worshippers to sing the words with full integrity. The English text attempts to keep some of the deep passion of the original but allow for wider use.

N.B. The guitar chords do not correspond exactly to the harmonised arrangement.

Words :   from the *Misa Popular Nicaraguense*;
English text © 1991 Iona Community.
Tune :   from the *Misa Popular Nicaraguense*;
arrangement © 1991 Iona Community.

KYRIE GUARANY
PARAGUAY

1. Oré mboriajú verekó Ñandeyara.

2. Oré mboriajú verekó Jesucristo.

1. On the poor, on the poor,
   show your mercy, O Lord.

2. On the poor, on the poor,
   show your mercy, O Christ.

Paraguay is the only country in Southern America which has its own indigenous language. The Guarany are the most oppressed people living on the east coast of Southern America and this song is their own. They are a very mild people, which is partly the reason for them being scattered throughout the sub-continent, sometimes led by Messiah figures and looking for a 'land without evils.'

Their *Kyrie* is slow and plaintive.

Words : adapted traditional liturgical text.
Music : as taught by Pablo Sosa:
arrangement © 1991 Iona Community.

GLORIA
PERU

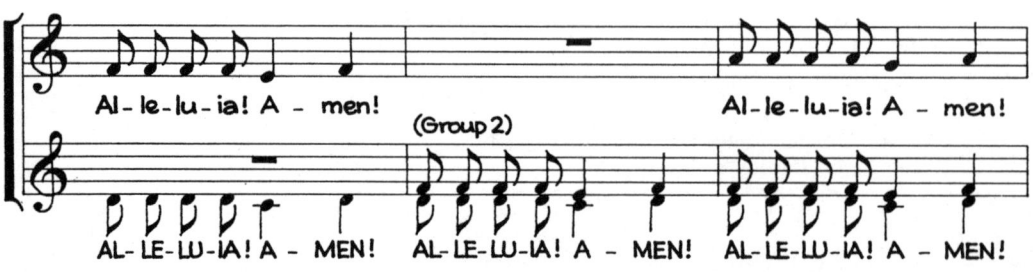

Cantor:	**Glory to God, glory to God, glory in the highest!**
ALL:	**GLORY TO GOD, GLORY TO GOD, GLORY IN THE HIGHEST!**
Cantor:	**To God be glory forever!**
ALL:	**TO GOD BE GLORY FOREVER!**
Cantor:	**Alleluia! Amen!**
Group 1:	**ALLELUIA! AMEN!**
Cantor:	**Alleluia! Amen!**
Groups 1, 2:	**ALLELUIA! AMEN!**
Cantor:	**Alleluia! Amen!**
Groups 1, 2, 3:	**ALLELUIA! AMEN!**
ALL:	**ALLELUIA! AMEN! ALLELUIA! AMEN!**

The city of Lima in Peru gives its name to a liturgy, prepared by the World Council of Churches in consultation with the Roman Catholic Church. The significance of the Lima Liturgy is that it is accepted as a valid form of the celebration of the Eucharist by the major worldwide denominations.

This *Gloria* is fondly associated with the Lima Liturgy and is a joy to sing whether or not Holy Communion is being celebrated.

What is required is that the congregation should be divided into three groups. When the cantor comes to the *alleluias*, he or she sings the lowest line and the first congregational group repeats it continually while the cantor gives the second group its line and the third group its line. The whole company then sing two more *alleluias*.

N.B. The above should not be taken as holy writ. There is immense variety in the ways this *Gloria* has been and can be sung.

Words: traditional liturgical text.
Music: traditional.

1. Let heaven your wonders proclaim,
   let angels your faithfulness praise,
   for who in the heights or the depths
   can equal your majesty, O God?

2. Your strength rules the rage of the sea,
   your faithfulness calms its wild waves,
   you quell every terror of the deep
   and scatter your enemies afar.

3. The heavens are yours and the earth:
   you founded the world and its wealth;
   the north and the south show your skill,
   the east and the west attest your fame.

4. Toughness and valour are yours,
   strong is your hand lifted high;
   yet justice is found at your throne
   and love is forever by your side.

5. So, glad are the people who praise you,
   who walk in the light of your love;
   in you, God alone, is their strength,
   their honour, their justice and their joy.

This beautiful and simple melody, though recently composed by Salvador Martinez, is perfectly in keeping with the texture of Philippino folk tunes. It can be sung quite satisfactorily with a simple guitar accompaniment. The harmonisation and arrangement are not indigenous.

Words: Psalm 89, text selected from vs. 1 – 16;
paraphrase © 1991 Iona Community.
Music: © 1989 Salvador T. Martinez;
arrangement © 1991 Iona Community.

LOVING CREATOR
PHILIPPINES

1. Loving Creator,
   grant to your children
   mercy and blessing,
   songs never ceasing,
   grace to invite us,
   peace to unite us —
   Loving Creator,
   parent and God.

2. Jesus Redeemer,
   help us remember
   your pain and passion,
   your resurrection,
   your call to follow,
   your love tomorrow —
   Jesus Redeemer,
   our friend and Lord.

3. Spirit descending,
   your light, unending,
   brings hope and healing,
   is truth revealing.
   Dispel our blindness,
   inspire our kindness —
   Spirit descending,
   Spirit adored.

It is slightly cheating to call this a Philippino song. The melody certainly comes from the Philippines, but the words are the product of the late D. T. Niles. Born in Ceylon (now Sri Lanka), D. T. Niles was a great ecumenist as well as hymnwriter and for a while was a president of the World Council of Churches.

Words : D. T. Niles;
© Christian Conference of Asia.
Music : *Halad*, by Elena G. Maquiso,
© Christian Conference of Asia;
arrangement © 1991 Iona Community.

MARANATHA
PHILIPPINES

We believe:
Maranatha, Light of the Day.

This very simple chant can be used before worship begins, as a quiet processional, to precede or follow the Gospel or wherever an affirmation is required.

The chant can be sung by groups of single or mixed genders divided equally and not according to part (soprano, alto etc.)

Words : from Revelation 22 vv. 5, 20.
Music : © 1991 Francisco Feliciano & Asian Institute of Liturgy and Music.

THE EARTH IS THE LORD'S
PHILIPPINES

at a walking pace

Lord, your hands have formed this world, eve-ry part is shaped by you— wa-ter tumb-ling o-ver rocks, air and sun-light: each day's signs that you make all things new.

Chords: E F#m7 B E C#m7 B E C#m F#m7 B7 E C#m F#m7 B7 E F#m7 B7 E

1. Lord, your hands have formed this world,
   every part is shaped by you —
   water tumbling over rocks, air and sunlight:
   each day's signs that you make all things new.

2. Yours the soil that holds the seed,
   you give warmth and moisture too.
   Sprouting blossoms, crops and buds, trees and plants:
   the season's signs that you make all things new.

3. Like a mat you roll out land,
   space to build, for us and you
   earthly homes and, better still, homes for Christ:
   the truest sign that you make all things new.

2a. Sweet potatoes fill our bags,
    when the garden yields its due.
    Chickens run and pigs grow plump, children too:
    your bounty's signs that you make all things new.

2b. We search out new ground to weed,
    even mountain fields will do.
    You uproot the toughest sins from our souls:
    both steward signs that you make all things new.

In these words, the authors claim the right to incarnate the Gospel not in an imported European or North American culture, but in the culture of people who work the soil. This is typical of much of the liturgy being developed in the Philippines where a conscious effort is made not to mimic Western models, but to provide words which are authentic in that historical and geographical situation.

Verses 2a and 2b are not expected to be sung by Westerners for whom the activities represented are alien.

Words : © 1991 Ramon and Sario Oliano;
paraphrase by James Minchin;
translation by Delebert Rice.
Music : *Gayom Ni Higami*, a traditional Ikalahan melody;
arrangement © 1991 Iona Community.

ALABANZA
PUERTO RICA

brightly
Nou-rished by the rain-fall, the earth can come a-live; wood-lands swell with
Flowers of eve-ry col-our now raise their heads in pride, prais-ing God their

Em B7 Em

splen-dour, the moors and mea-dows thrive.   EACH FLOWER HAS ITS
ma-ker through-out the coun-try-side.   ALL, ALL OF CRE-

Am7 B7 Em E E7

PUR-POSE, AND EVE-RY PE-TAL ITS PLACE,   EACH CE-LE-BRATES
-A-TION DE-LIGHTS TO WOR-SHIP THE LORD.   LET THOSE IN GOD'S

Am7 D D7 G C

1. Nourished by the rainfall, the earth can come alive;
   woodlands swell with splendour, the moors and meadows thrive.
   Flowers of every colour now raise their heads in pride,
   praising God their maker throughout the countryside.

   **EACH FLOWER HAS ITS PURPOSE, AND EVERY PETAL ITS PLACE,
   EACH CELEBRATES GLORY, EACH SPEAKS OF GOD'S GOOD GRACE.
   ALL, ALL OF CREATION DELIGHTS TO WORSHIP THE LORD.
   LET THOSE IN GOD'S IMAGE RESPOND IN DEED AND WORD.**

2. Birds that wake the morning and fill the evening sky
   sing not to please humans, but to praise God on high.
   Nightingale and curlew, the robin, rook and wren,
   first rehearse their anthem, then sing it through again.

   **EACH BIRD HAS ITS PURPOSE, AND EVERY SONG HAS ITS PLACE, . . .
   EACH CELEBRATES GLORY, EACH SPEAKS OF GOD'S GOOD GRACE.
   ALL, ALL OF CREATION DELIGHTS TO WORSHIP THE LORD.
   LET THOSE IN GOD'S IMAGE RESPOND IN DEED AND WORD.**

3. Sea in endless churning, the sky in endless girth,
   land in endless contour, and life in endless birth,
   hilltop near the city, a stone beside a tomb,
   all bear silent witness to him who made earth bloom.

   EACH HILL HAS ITS PURPOSE, AND EVERY STONE HAS ITS PLACE, . . .
   EACH CELEBRATES GLORY, EACH SPEAKS OF GOD'S GOOD GRACE.
   ALL, ALL OF CREATION DELIGHTS TO WORSHIP THE LORD.
   LET THOSE IN GOD'S IMAGE RESPOND IN DEED AND WORD.

4. Every land and nation, each woman, child and man,
   find their root and reason before the world began;
   all by God were destined to hear the Saviour's call
   and choose to give him nothing or gladly give him all.

   EACH SOUL HAS ITS PURPOSE, AND EVERY CHILD HAS ITS PLACE, . . .
   EACH CELEBRATES GLORY, EACH SPEAKS OF GOD'S GOOD GRACE.
   ALL, ALL OF CREATION DELIGHTS TO WORSHIP THE LORD.
   LET THOSE IN GOD'S IMAGE RESPOND IN DEED AND WORD.

1. *Al caer la lluvia resurge con verdor*
   toda la floresta, renueva la creación!
   Mira el rojo lirio, el duende ya brotó.
   Bella primavera que anuncia su fulgor!

Chorus: **TODA FLOR SILVESTRE, LA MAYA, EL CUNDEAMOR . . .**
CÓMO MANIFIESTAN LA GLORIA DEL SEÑOR!
CÓMO SE TE ALABA TODA LA CREACIÓN!
YO QUISIERA HACERLO EN FORMA IGUAL, SEÑOR.

2. *El "coquí" se alegra, se siente muy feliz . . .*
   Canta en su alabanza: "coquí, coquí, coquí."
   El pitirre canta y trina el ruiseñor
   Cuán alegremente alaban al Creador!

The Spanish text is not here translated literally, as it alludes to flowers and birds native to Puerto Rica which may not be common elsewhere. The song is, in origin, a celebration of spring. The English text allows for the song to be used all year round in celebration of God's providence.

Words :   © 1991 Pablo Fernandez Badillo.
         translation © 1991 Iona Community.
Music :   © 1991 Pablo Fernandez Badillo.

ALLELUIA
SOUTH AFRICA

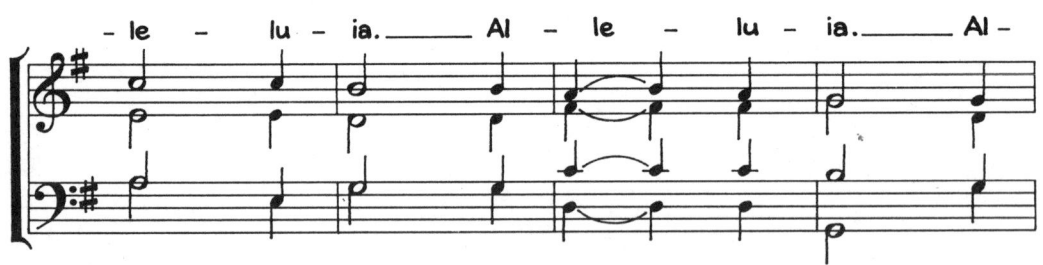
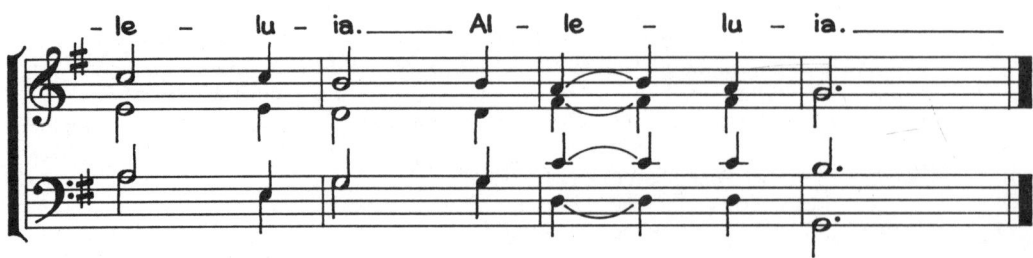

Alleluia.

A chance look at a video recording of a service in a black South African church led to this melody being transcribed. The *Alleluia* was being led by George Mxadana who sang a beautiful melismatic line as the congregation took up the four-part harmony.

The *Alleluia* should not be sung with too much vigour. In this setting, it is more a meditative affirmation than a loud shout.

Words : traditional liturgical text.
Music : as transcribed from the singing of George Mxadana.

BAYAVUYA
SOUTH AFRICA

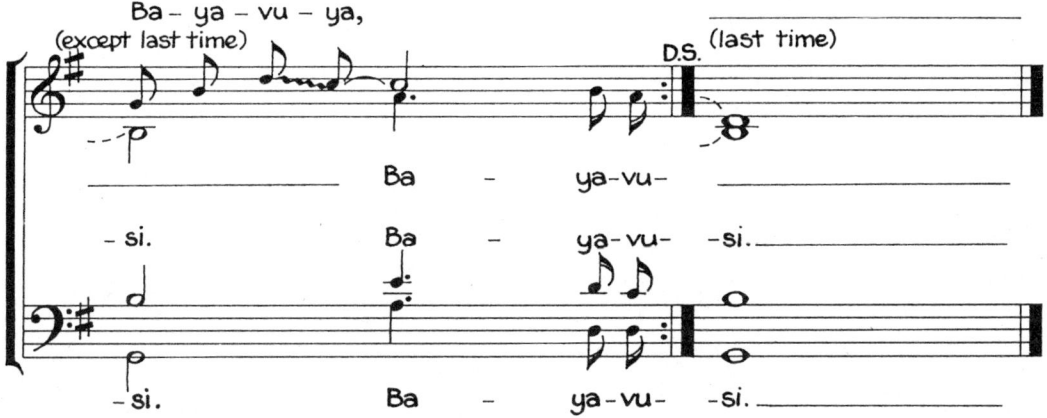

Bayavuy' abantu bahko.
Isabatha namhla Nkosi.

Lord, your people are happy.

This song should be sung quite lazily. The squiggles in the soprano line before each final note of the bar indicates a slide from the penultimate note down. Nothing more than this is known about the song. It was taken down at an *ad hoc* concert at which a nun from Soweto began to sing it, the harmony coming from other South Africans in her immediate vicinity.

Words : source unknown.
Music : traditional;
as taught by Sr. Monica Mothile,
arrangement © 1991 Iona Community.

RE YA MATHEMATHA
SOUTH AFRICA

*Re ya mathematha,
re ya gae Jerusalema.*

We're running home to Jerusalem.

Throughout the world, there are songs about running, marching, coming back home to or making for Jerusalem (or Zion). For some people the words may be an indication of their commitment to Christ and turning their backs on their old ways; for others the words may speak of a longing for heaven; for others yet, talk of Jerusalem may have political overtones in the same way as Babylon has.

Whatever the original intention of this song, it is very lively and enjoyable to sing. The language is Tswana and the song was transcribed in 1989 by Maggie Hamilton, an English musician who spent a while in South Africa listening to the songs of various black peoples.

The top line of music is sung by the cantor or leader.

Words : traditional (Tswana).
Music : traditional;
transcribed from the singing of the youth group of Ebenezer Evangelical Church, Mohlakeng, Randfontein by Maggie Hamilton, June 1989.

SENZENI NA
SOUTH AFRICA

Senzeni na, senzeni na,
senzeni na, senzeni na,
senzeni na, senzeni na,
senzeni na, senzeni na?

Sono sethu, sono sethu,
sono sethu, sono sethu,
sono sethu, sono sethu,
sono sethu, sono sethu?

What have we done?

What is our sin?

This song might almost be described as the national anthem of suffering people. It has been sung throughout South Africa whenever the marginalised have needed to share their pain with God or with each other. It is also used as a protest song.

There is a third verse which answers the first two and means 'We are black', but it would be impossible for white Westeners to sing that with the conviction it requires.

Words : traditional.
Music : traditional.

THUMA MINA
SOUTH AFRICA

1. *Thuma mina, thuma mina,
   thuma mina, Nkosi yam.*

2. *Ndiya vuma, ndiya vuma,
   ndiya vuma, Nkosi yam.*

1. Send me, Jesus; send me, Jesus;
   send me, Jesus; send me, Lord.

2. I am willing; I am willing;
   I am willing, willing, Lord.

This is a transcription of a beautiful South African song of discipleship. It is very easy to teach the harmony and once people sing it, they don't forget it. A good time to use the song is at the end of a meeting as people are preparing to go. It can be used as a recessional, getting louder or quieter as the mood requires.

Words : traditional.
Music : traditional;
transcribed from the singing of Lulu Dumazweni;
arrangement © 1991 Iona Community.

CH'IU CHU LIENMIN WOMEN
TAIWAN

slowly and deliberately

Ch'iu Chu lien-min wo-men.
Lord, have mer-cy on us.

Ch'iu Chi-tu lien-min wo-men.
Christ, have mer-cy on us.

Ch'iu Chu lien-min wo-men.
Lord, have mer-cy on us.

Ch'iu Chu lienmin women.
Ch'iu Chitu lienmin women.
Ch'iu Chu lienmin women.

Lord, have mercy on us.
Christ, have mercy on us.
Lord, have mercy on us.

This very simple *Kyrie* is frequently used by the World Council of Churches at conferences. For its best effect, a large orchestral gong should be struck at the end of each singing.

There is no time signature. The music should move slowly without rigidity, somewhat like a plainsong melody.

Words : traditional liturgical text.
Music : © 1991 I-to Loh.

IF YOU BELIEVE AND I BELIEVE

ZIMBABWE

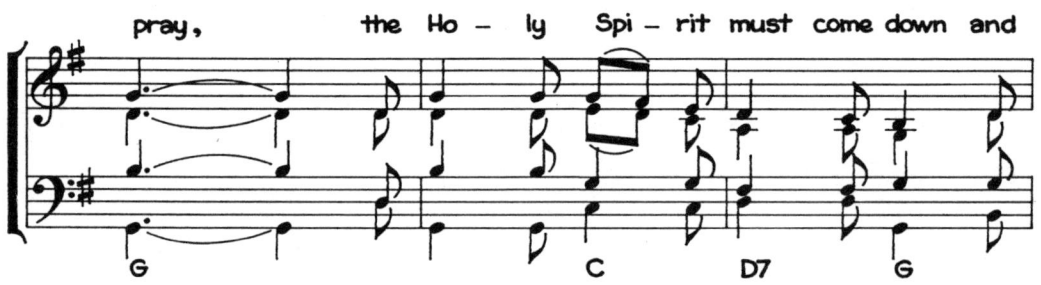

If you believe and I believe
and we together pray,
the Holy Spirit must come down
and set God's people free,
and set God's people free,
and set God's people free;
the Holy Spirit must come down
and set God's people free.

Those who are familiar with English folksong might find it strange that this melody should be attributed to Zimbabwe. That is because this is a beautiful example of righteous subversiveness.

The tune is a derivation of *The Lincolnshire Poacher*. The possibility is that the song was taken by English settlers or traders to Southern Rhodesia (as was) and the tune picked up by servants. In the course of time, the tune became altered and allied to words expressing a very strong anti-colonial sentiment.

During the fight for independance, black people native to the colony sang the above words, but in their original version, for 'God's people' read 'Zimbabwe'. The song became a hymn of entreaty and defiance.

It was sung to us by a Zimbabwian woman who, at a conference in 1985 was so moved by the plight of a sister delegate from Namibia that she sang the song, substituting 'Namibia' for 'Zimbabwe'.

If the song is part of intercessory prayer for a particular country, it is perfectly reasonable to follow the practice of naming the country rather than singing 'God's people'.

Words :   Zimbabwean traditional.
Music :   Zimbabwean traditional (adapted from English source) as taught by Tarasai.

ACKNOWLEDGEMENTS

Overleaf are listed the copyright holders of various items in this collection. Permission to reproduce must be obtained from them whenever appropriate. Translation of words copyright the Iona Community may be freely reproduced for one-off non commercial purposes as long as appropriate acknowledgement is made.

In thanking the copyright holders for granting permission for words and music to be printed, we also wish to record our very deep gratitude to people throughout the world who have, by their effort and encouragement, helped this book to move from hope to a reality. In particular we are indebted to:

Terry MacArthur & Jorge Maldonado   —   World Council of Churches.
Pablo Sosa   —   Argentina.
Salvador Martinez   —   Philippines and Hong Kong.
George Mxadana, Monica Mothile & Lulu Dumazweni   —   South Africa.
Tarasai   —   Zimbabwe.
Maggie Hamilton   —   England.
David Lacey   —   Scotland.
Dougie and Linda Small   —   Scotland.
Members of the Wild Goose Worship Group   —   Scotland.
Maggie Simpson   —   Secretary.
Michael Lee   —   Publications Manager.

COPYRIGHT HOLDERS

ARGENTINA
El cielo canta — Pablo Sosa, Buenos Aires, Argentina.

BOLIVIA
Sarantañani — Zoilo Yanapa, La Paz, Bolivia.

BRAZIL
Cantai ao Senhor — Editora Sinodal, Sao Leopoldo, Brazil.

CANADA
Jesous Ahatonhia — words: used by permission of Frederick Harris Music Co. Ltd., 529 Speers Road, Oakville, Ontario, Canada. All rights reserved.

CHINA
Wen Ti — Abingdon Press, 201 Eighth Avenue S., Nashville, TN. 37702, U.S.A. From *Hymns From the Four Winds*. Used by permission.

GERMANY
Gelobt sei deine Treu — Joachim Klepper, Germany.

GREECE
Kyrie eleison — origin unknown.

KOREA
Come now, O Prince of peace — Geonyong Lee, Seoul, South Korea.
Look and Learn — Nah Young-Soo, Seoul, South Korea.

NICARAGUA
Sent by the Lord — translation: Jorge Maldonado, W.C.C., Geneva, Switzerland.
Somos pueblo que camina — Misa Popular Nicaraguense.

PARAGUAY
Kyrie Guarany — origin unknown.

PERU
Gloria — origin unknown.

PHILIPPINES
Let heaven your wonders proclaim — Salvador T. Martinez, Kowloon, Hong Kong.

Loving Creator — Christian Conference of Asia,
c/o Asian Institute for Liturgy and Music,
P. O. Box 3167, Manila 1099,
Philippines.
Maranatha — Francisco Feliciano & Asian Institute for Liturgy and Music, Quezon City, Philippines.
The earth is the Lord's — Words: Ramon & Sario Oliano, Philippines, and others.

PUERTO RICA
Alabanza — Pablo Fernandez Badillo, Puerto Rica.

SOUTH AFRICA
Alleluia — origin unknown.
Bayavuya — origin unknown.
Re ya mathematha — origin unknown.
Senzeni na — origin unknown.
Thuma Mina — origin unknown.

TAIWAN
Ch'iu Chu lienmin women — I-to Loh, Manilla.

ZIMBABWE
If you believe and I believe — origin unknown.

COPYRIGHT

All translations of original texts and arrangements of original music are copyright the Iona Community.

While every effort has been made to identify the sources and copyright holders of materials included, the compilers would be grateful to know of information which may help to rectify details of origin etc.

Where copyright holders have been identified, the appropriate proportion of copyright fee recovered from the sale of this book will be sent to them. Where no copyright holder has been identified, the appropriate proportion of the copyright fee will be sent to the Council of Churches in the designated country.

ALPHABETICAL INDEX OF FIRST LINES

54	Al caer la lluvia resurge con verdor
58	Alleluia
60	Bayavuy' abantu bahko
14	Cantai ao Senhor um cantico novo
70	Ch'iu Chu lienmin women
26	Come now, O Prince of peace
10	El cielo canta alegría, aleluia!
36	*For the world and all its people*
22	Gelobt sei deine Treu
40	Glory to God, glory to God
22	*'Glory to God on high'*
10	*Heaven is singing for joy, alleluia!*
72	If you believe and I believe
24	Kyrie eleison
42	Let heaven your wonders proclaim
28	Look and learn from the birds of the air
24	*Lord, have mercy*
70	*Lord, have mercy on us*
52	Lord, your hands have formed this world
46	Loving Creator
20	May the Lord, mighty God
12	*Men and women, let us walk*
54	*Nourished by the rainfall, the earth can come alive*
14	*O sing to the Lord, O sing God a new song*
38	On the poor, on the poor
38	Oré mboriajú verekó Ñandeyara
62	Re ya mathematha
68	*Send me, Jesus; send me, Jesus*
32	Sent by the Lord am I
66	Senzeni na, senzeni na
36	Somos pueblo que camina
12	Tatanaca, mamanaca, Sarantañani!
68	Thuma mina, thuma mina
16	'Twas in the moon of wintertime
50	We believe
22	*When morning meets our eyes*

Words in italics indicate a popular English translation of the original text.

79